Photography by:
Hugo van Lawick, Günter Ziesler, Leslie Groff,
Maratea, John Wightman, Wardene Weisser,
Toni Beamish, Clem Haagner, Pat Morris.

ELEPHANT FAMILY
Jane Goodall

A MADISON MINI BOOK

Published by Madison Marketing Limited.
Madison Marketing Limited holds the exclusive
license to this edition.
Copyright © 1991 by Neugebauer Rights & Licenses AG., Zurich.
Text copyright © 1991 by Jane Goodall.
All rights reserved.
ISBN 1-55066-017-9

Printed in Canada

Printed on recycled paper

ELEPHANT FAMILY

Jane Goodall
ANIMAL SERIES

*P*hotographs selected by
Michael Neugebauer

Madison Marketing Limited

*I*t is truly amazing to see how an elephant can destroy a whole tree. This huge female is called Mama. She reaches high up with her trunk, curls it around a branch – and pulls. Crack! She pulls it down. Nearby some of her family work on another tree. An elephant can even knock a big tree over just by pushing with his head.

Mama makes a rumbling sound of pleasure. Winding her trunk around a branch, she strips off the leaves and pops them into her mouth. Soon other elephants come to share the leaves that none of them could reach before. They are Mama's sisters and aunts and her eldest daughter. Mama is the leader of this family group.

One of the females, Hazel, has twin sons named Horace and Henry. They stay close to their mother as she feeds. Horace curls his trunk back out of the way and suckles from one of the two teats between Hazel's front legs. It's not often that twin elephants are born, so we're observing this pair carefully. Two of the Tanzanian park rangers follow these elephants almost every day.

The elephants feed peacefully until a nine-year-old male named Oscar tries to join in. One of the females threatens him, tossing her head and trunk and flapping her huge ears. He stands his ground so she charges at him, trumpeting. Oscar runs off. He stops and watches the females for a while, then chases off after a bird. When Oscar is about 13 he'll leave his family group and join some adult males. The big males only travel with family groups when one of the females is ready to start a baby.

The elephants move towards a water hole. They find five big males there. One of them is the oldest elephant I have ever seen. His name is Kibiyongo. His teeth are worn away, his ears have drooped and his skin has fallen in wrinkles around his ankles. His companions often help him. Sometimes they hold down branches so he can feed on the soft leaves at the end.

Elephants always try to help companions who are very old or sick or wounded. They grieve when a group member dies, and cover the body with branches and earth. They are very intelligent and their feelings seem to be much like ours.

Kibiyongo and the other males greet the females, gently touching their mouths and behind their ears with their trunks. And then the elephants really start to enjoy themselves. They suck up water and squirt it into their mouths. They lie down in the mud and cover their skins. They squirt water over themselves. The little ones play, charging about with outstretched ears and trumpeting loudly.

Kibiyongo and his friends soon leave, gleaming with wet, black mud. Mama and her family rest in the shade. The little ones suckle, then stretch out, with some of the adults standing around protectively. One of the females rests her trunk over her tusks.

In the old days, when the elephants roamed for miles and miles, the damage they did to the trees didn't matter much. There were many more trees, and, slowly, new ones grew. Today it is different. There are so many people. There is less and less room for elephants. When they kill the trees where they live there is nowhere else for them to go.

In the cool of the evening the elephants stop to feed again. Another family group appears, moving silently on huge feet. The leaders of the two groups greet, twining their trunks. There are many more greetings. Oscar charges an elephant of the same age from the other group. They trumpet loudly and there is a clashing of tusks. Then Oscar, who is a bit bigger, chases the other away.

Gradually they calm down. The twins suckle. The tiny baby keeps very close to his mother, often standing right underneath her. It is very peaceful. When I drive away, they are all feeding quietly together, dark shadows in the last light of evening.

*J*ANE GOODALL has shared her important discoveries and her love of animals with millions of people around the world through books, films and lectures. She has founded ongoing research and educational institutes on two continents, and is one of the world's most acclaimed naturalists.

The Jane Goodall Institute for Wildlife
Research, Education and Conservation
P.O. Box 41720, Tucson, AZ 85717 U.S.A.

The Jane Goodall Institute — Canada
P.O. Box 3125, Station "C"
Ottawa, Ontario K1Y 4J4 Canada

The Jane Goodall Institute — U.K.
15 Clarendon Park
Lymington, Hants SO41 8AX United Kingdom